putting parenting to bed

uncommon sense for modern parents

Leader's Guide

Putting Parenting to Bed: Leader's guide

© Ann Benton/The Good Book Company 2008

Published by The Good Book Company

Elm House, 37 Elm Road, New Malden, Surrey KT3 3HB, UK

Tel: 020-8942-0880; Fax: 020-8942-0990

E-mail: admin@thegoodbook.co.uk

website: www.thegoodbook.co.uk

ISBN: 9781905564224

Cover design by Carl Hamblin

Printed in the UK

CONTENTS

INTRODUCTION

Do we need another course on parenting?

Advice for parents is everywhere. Just have a look in any high-street bookshop, or ask a health visitor. So why another course? This parenting course is different in a number of ways:

1. It runs for only three sessions

Most parenting courses run for six or even ten weeks, and demand a high level of commitment from people at a very busy time of life. If both parents attend—and ideally that is best—a lot of baby-sitting will be needed. Past experience shows that many parents are more willing to commit to a course which takes only three sessions. And although each session covers a lot of ground, parents won't mind being stretched a little, as long as there is a good sense of pace, purpose and achievement.

This course aims to help parents to be confident in their role. A lengthy parenting course can give the impression that raising children is a difficult thing, which requires extraordinary expertise, like growing prize dahlias or upholstering a sofa. But if we make the whole process unnecessarily difficult and mysterious, it will only undermine any confidence that parents might have.

It is also possible to run this course in six shorter sessions, and this could certainly be more practical if the course is held during the day and accompanied by a crèche.

2. It follows simple, common sense principles

Many longer courses contain a lot of 'popular psychology'—insights or ideas that purport to show why we do things. This might be fascinating to some people, but it's not essential for successfully bringing up children; many parents have raised perfectly decent human beings, without any instruction in 'anger management' or 'self-esteem'.

In fact, one of the aims of this course is to show that raising children is an ordinary, everyday process, which depends on following just a few common-sense principles. This course is based on three of these principles:

- parents should have **loving authority** over their children
- parents should exercise **loving discipline** with their children
- parents should enjoy a **loving relationship** with their children

3. It is not afraid to be directive

This parenting course looks to the Bible and the Christian faith for principles. It is shaped by the fact that Christians are quite comfortable with the idea of receiving wisdom from outside ourselves—this, after all, is precisely how people become Christians and receive God's salvation. So this course will be directive when it comes to principles; it will say that this is the best way for everybody because it reflects the way our Maker built us. We are made in God's image, so good parenting will reflect how God parents his own children. He does this with loving authority and loving discipline; all in the context of a loving relationship, which he calls people into through Jesus Christ.

By contrast, most parenting courses, although they contain a lot of good sense, do not tend to use 'ought' and 'must'; they are 'non-directive'. Rather, they argue along the lines of 'how would you like it?' Advice is usually based on reflection and self-evaluation, and aims to prove that a particular route feels nicer all round. This course, while recognising that such an approach can sometimes be helpful, refers far more frequently to the idea that some things are right and others are wrong, in a way that is quite independent of our feelings.

Interestingly, even people who have no belief in God willingly accept this kind of 'wisdom from outside', even when they may not believe in anyone 'outside'. That is something that the course will gently point out as one piece of evidence that we were made by God and for him.

Past experience shows that parents who are confused by all the advice available today are quite glad to learn some received wisdom, and will accept that the Bible is at least as good a place to get it from as anywhere else.

the opportunity to make the material their own—for instance, space is provided for leaders to insert their own illustrations, either from personal experience or from current events. If the course leader is confident enough about speaking publicly, the advantage of using an outline (as opposed to a script) is that the talk is more likely to be spoken, rather than read to the audience.

Scripts of these talks, as originally given, are also available for download from The Good Book Company website. The person who teaches this course may use these scripts verbatim if they prefer.

It might be good to have two speakers, one male and one female, at each session, and to divide the material up between them. Some men may be more receptive to the voice and experience of a fellow dad. Mothers and fathers each bring something special and different to the home, not least a perspective which is gender-linked. While the Bible clearly teaches that there is a difference between male and female, husbands and wives, and mothers and fathers, that is not an issue on which this course majors. For an excellent treatment of the specific role of fathers see *Fatherhood* by Tony Payne, available from The Good Book Company.

Group activities and discussions

Every session includes a number of discussion slots when the parents are encouraged to answer some questions together. Where a larger number of people attend (more than eight, say), it would be helpful to arrange small groups around a number of tables. This gives an air of informality, allows everyone to be included, and automatically provides a structure for group discussion.

The first of the interludes in each of the three sessions is very much an ice-breaker. The discussion relates to an extract from a film; the three specifically suggested in this course are *Parenthood*, *The Sound of Music*, and *Dead Poets Society*. All of these movies are still available to hire, buy or download. However, as a course leader, you might find better or more current examples to use in place of those recommended. A resume of the extract is included, so that the leader will be able to locate it in the film. These extracts last only two to three minutes, but they are an enjoyable way to begin and introduce the concept of the session.

ing about other activities or courses which the church offers.

Because there are always new parents in the community, it is worth considering running *Putting Parenting to Bed* **on an annual basis.**

It is the hope of those who have produced this course that many parents will not only appreciate and follow the wisdom of the Bible, but that they will come to know Christ, in whom are hidden all the treasures of wisdom and knowledge. Therefore, as churches, we need to be ready to receive seekers (and their children) among us, with all the implications which that may have for resources, manpower and patience.

To God alone be glory.

Ann Benton, February 2008

1: THE TROUBLE WITH PARENTING—PARENTS!

Please read these notes ahead of time and use them to ensure that you are well-prepared for leading the session.

Key concept:
Loving authority

Theological basis:
God is our Maker; He made everything beautiful and good. He made each human a living soul. But although we have innate dignity and significance, we are utterly fallible and frail. We mess up!

Gospel opportunity:
Only the Bible can explain what we instinctively feel to be true, that every child born is precious. Only the Bible can explain why the world is both beautiful and awful, and why human beings can recognise what is good and yet fail to do it.

Preparing for Session 1

★ **Getting in:** Put yourself in the shoes of those attending this first session, especially if they are new to the building where the course is held. Start by standing outside. Is it obvious that this is where the course will be run? Does the entrance look warm, light and inviting? Will you station someone outside to act as a welcomer?

Trace their journey into the building and make sure that it will be clear where they are to go. You may like to think about some signs that will confirm they are in the right place and help them to find their way around. Think about organising a couple of helpers who can welcome people at the entrances to the building and the room itself. First impressions are really important: will their first impression be a good one?

★ **Organising the room:** Think carefully about how you will organise the room where you are meeting. It is a good idea to reserve some seats at the back or near the entrance for the inevitable latecomers, to avoid making them walk right across a room full of strangers when the session has already started. Alternatively, organise someone to sit near the entrance and look out for latecomers. Be realistic about the number of seats that you provide—people can feel quite uncomfortable if there are only a small number of participants in a room that has been organised to seat multitudes! On the other hand, make sure that extra seats are easily available, in case more people turn up than expected. Think about having some background music on when people arrive, and having some simple decorations on the tables.

★ **Refreshments:** If possible, organise someone to take charge of refreshments, so that you, as course leader, are free to spend time with your 'students'.

★ **Resources:** Make sure you have sufficient copies of the *Putting Parenting to Bed Study Guide* and plenty of pens for people to use. You may also like to set out one or more of the following, on each group's table or elsewhere in the room:

- Printed details of your church
- Details of an evangelistic course
- Details of a future evangelistic event
- Some Bibles
- Evangelistic leaflets
- Christian literature on family issues, appropriate for non-Christians
- Paper for people to write down questions
- A question box.

★ **Technology:** If you are using the film extract, make sure that it is set up for viewing and that curtains or blinds can quickly be drawn, or are already closed at the beginning of the session. Check the visibility and audibility before people arrive. If you are using powerpoint to project headings or points – check that it runs smoothly, and that laptops have sufficient battery power, or are plugged in!

★ **Important information:** Make a list of any items of information that you may need to pass on to the group, such as fire emergency instructions, location of the toilets, local parking restrictions etc. Deliver this information quickly at the start, without too much fuss, before you get straight on to the main subject.

★ **Remembering names:** People appreciate it if you can remember their names, so you may find it helpful to have a piece of paper handy on which you can note down the names of your 'students'. For your own reference, if the group is large, you could draw a diagram of the tables in the room, and note down the names of people where they are sitting. People are likely to sit in the same place for subsequent sessions, so this may help you to remember who everyone is. Alternatively, you could provide sticky labels and marker pens each week for impromptu name badges.

★ **Know your notes:** Make sure you are familiar with the *Presentation Notes* for Session 1 (see p. 19), so that you can speak freely to your audience, as opposed to reading to them. A version of the full text is available on www.thegoodbook.co.uk in MS Word for download. Adapt the scripts using your own illustrations. Think carefully also about the various gospel opportunities that may present themselves during this session. Rather than scripting such comments, it's better to keep the Christian angle constantly in mind, so that you can mention these points as and when appropriate.

★ **Pastoral care:** One of the group discussions in this session will touch on parents' own upbringing. There is the possibility that someone may reveal painful personal issues arising from an abusive or neglectful upbringing. You ought to think about how someone like this could be helped, should they reveal a need. You may need to speak to a leader in your church about this kind of issue, as part of your preparation for this course.

★ **Timing:** Plan the timing of each part of the session, and try not to overrun your schedule by more than five minutes, otherwise it will become very difficult to catch up and finish on time. See a suggested schedule for Session 1 on page 18.

Note: Session 1 may take slightly longer than other sessions because of the need to introduce everything and give people time to settle down.

If you are doing the course in 6 sessions, then finish at the Refreshment break. Session 2 will begin with the 2nd group discussion.

Introduction and time to settle down	*15 minutes*
Film extract and discussion	*15 minutes*
Presentation 1	*25 minutes*
Refreshments and toilet break	*5 minutes*
Group discussion 2	*10 minutes*
Presentation 2	*25 minutes*
Group discussion 3	*10 minutes*
Wrap up	*5 minutes*
Total	**1 hour 50 minutes**

Aims of Session 1

A: What is a child?

- To introduce the course and outline what will be covered in the next three (or six) sessions.

- To get parents chatting comfortably with each other about their children and their own parenting.

- To reassure parents that it is normal to feel guilty about inadequate parenting.

- To expose as an error the idea that 'all you need is love'.

- To examine various commonplace ideas about what a child is, with the aim of evaluating each one and thinking about the implications for parenting.

B: Parenting pitfalls

- To help parents understand that the key to tackling many parenting problems is not changing the child so much as changing the parent.

- To expose some of the common errors that loving parents fall into, and to help them understand how to improve their parenting.

- To reassure people that, despite the fact that there is no such thing as a perfect parent, with love, understanding and a willingness to change, they are all able to be effective parents.

- To encourage parents to be confident in their God-given authority to parent, and to challenge them to take seriously their God-given responsibility to instruct and guide their children.

PRESENTATION NOTES FOR SESSION 1

Introduction (15 minutes maximum)

As this is the first session of the course, you will need to introduce yourself. In a small group (fewer than eight, say) you may also want to ask participants to introduce themselves. In a larger group, if you have organised people around tables, you may want to allow a few moments for people to introduce themselves to those sitting nearest to them.

- **Important information:** Welcome everybody and introduce yourself as leader of the course. Make sure people know their way around the building (Where are the toilets?) and give any other important information as necessary (car parking, fire emergency instructions etc).

- **An outline of the course:** Give an outline of the structure of the course (mentioning whether it is to be held over three or six sessions).

- **Study Guide:** Make sure that everyone has a copy of the Study Guide, and something to write with. Encourage parents to make notes in their Study Guide throughout the session.

- **Handling questions:** You may also want to specify how you will handle questions: Are people welcome to interject? Will you allocate a time slot specifically for questions in each session? Should people write down their questions or speak to you after the session?

- **Biblical basis:** Mention the fact that this course has been based on the teaching of the Bible—that will become apparent at certain points. This may well raise questions relating to the Christian faith, rather than parenting. Make sure that people know they are always welcome to ask such questions, but also ensure that everyone understands that these questions can't be answered during the session itself. Refer people to the Study Guide Introduction on p5 for more information.

- **The aims of the course:** Not to make parents feel bad about their failures in parenting. Instead...

  a. to help parents face up to their fears in raising children.

  b. to discover the important things from all the advice that parents receive.

  c. to encourage parents to get on with their responsibilities.

  (You could comment on the fact that vast amounts of advice for today's parents has only resulted in parents who are more confused, and children who are less well-adjusted. But reassure people that this course will be different!)

- **An outline of what you will cover in the session.**

Film extract (15 minutes with Group discussion 1)

The purpose of the film extract from Parenthood is to raise the issue of parental guilt and how we might try to cope with it. This is to help parents see that they are not alone in feeling guilty about their inadequacies or fearing for their child's future. It is important that you, as course leader, are not speaking to the parents from a great height of expertise. You can also enthuse them with the prospect that the insights and strategies learned on this course can help ordinary, imperfect people to carry out this awesome responsibility.

  The extract: The hapless parents are called into their son's school to discuss his unacceptable behaviour and poor performance. The principal says: *'I think we are going to have to be very careful about Kevin's educational environment.'*

  There follows a discussion of Kevin's 'emotional problems', and immediately the parents look for someone to blame.

  'She smoked grass!'

  'He lets them watch too much TV.'

- Talk about how you and most parents would feel on receiving a phone call from your child's head teacher, summoning them to a meeting to discuss your child's poor performance or unacceptable behaviour.

- Remind people of what was happening in the film extract—the parents got defensive and started blaming each other.

- Reassure people that all parents tend to feel guilty about inadequate parenting—this is an experience and reaction that all parents can identify with.

- Remind your group again that the purpose of this course is not to make them feel more guilty, but to give them insights and strategies that will help them to become better parents.

Note: If you can't find *Parenthood*, then there is a clip from *The Incredibles* that works just as well: kids running wild; Mum angry; Dad failing to engage.

Group discussion 1

Since the topic involves parents talking about their children, there shouldn't too much difficulty in getting people to talk. Give enough time for everyone to have an opportunity to speak. If you can see that one person is dominating, you may like to suggest from the front that each group ensures that they have heard from everybody. Give a couple of minutes' warning before you bring the group discussion to a close.

- Refer to p8 of Study Guide and draw attention to the discussion questions.

- Each parent introduces their child/children.

- Parents should say three things about their child/children that they find delightful or endearing.

- Parents should mention one thing about their child that they fear will result in an unwelcome appointment with the head teacher!

Presentation A: What is a child? (20-30 minutes)

Although it might appear academic at first sight, this opening subject is really important because, if we have an incorrect understanding of what a child actually is, we will inevitably have an incorrect view of what is involved in parenting. The presentation goes through a number of possible answers to this question; all have some currency in our society, all have implications for parenting, and some are contradictory—they can't all be correct!

Four of the answers—a random collection of atoms, a fashion accessory, a blank sheet of paper and genetically programmed—are incorrect or inadequate, and the problems of these views are highlighted in the talk. The other four answers—uniquely created, innocent, wayward and a gift from God—are based on biblical teaching, although this probably won't be apparent to non-

Christian parents. Don't be afraid to be explicit in informing them of this fact, especially as these are the views that the course adopts and refers to later on.

• •

Gospel Opportunity: People may be intrigued by the Christian view of children. You can take the opportunity to encourage them to discover for themselves where these ideas come from in the Bible, in whatever way is most appropriate. But don't try to make it a 'big deal' in the first session. The big idea of this first session is that parents need to exercise **loving authority.** There is an obvious chance to talk about how God is the pattern for true parenting.

• •

Outline of Presentation A:

Introductory comments

- Comment on what you could see of the parents' love for and enjoyment of their children as they talked about them in their groups.

- Question the belief that 'all you need is love' when it comes to bringing up children. Does lack of love explain every problem between parents and children? And what is true love anyway?

- Mention how the course will highlight issues that parents need to know and think about, that will inform and guide their love for their children.

- Introduce the question: *what is a child?* Refer to p9 of Study Guide. Point out the list of possible answers to this question given in the Study Guide (p 9-10). Give people a minute or two to read through them and circle those they agree with.

WHAT IS A CHILD?

1. A random collection of atoms/ chemicals

- **Implications:** we have no reason to say that a child is any more significant than any other natural object (eg: tree, cockroach).

- **Problem:** in reality, we don't treat our children as if they have no special significance. *(Give one or two illustrations eg: loss of a newborn baby, our response to film footage of hungry or sick babies in disaster areas, etc.)*

2. Uniquely created

- Point out ways in which we all regard children in this way (eg: the way people respond to a newborn infant, the way in which school teachers can get to know hundreds of children during their career, but never meet anyone who is an exact copy of another child etc.) Mention that this is the view of the Bible.

- **Implications:** we shouldn't be making comparisons between our child and their peers (give an illustration of how we commonly do this). Our child is worthy of being treated with utmost dignity and respect for what they are themselves.

3. Consumer item/ fashion accessory

- Describe how having a baby can be seen as the cherry on the cake for prosperous, middle-class, fashion-conscious couples who have acquired a good career, home, lifestyle and bank-balance. *(You may find an illustration of this in papers or magazines.)*

- **Problem:** how will people with this attitude view their children when those children are not convenient, or clever, or attractive, or when they have disabilities or emotional and behavioural problems?

- You could point out how this view of children has resulted in the disturbing contradiction of an increase in both abortions *and* fertility treatments, as women have come to expect the right to choose exactly when and how to have babies, to fit in with their careers and lifestyle.

4. Innocent

- Describe how we are struck by the innocence of a child eg: big eyes staring up at you from a cot, a small hand which reaches trustingly for yours, etc.

- What is innocence? Vulnerability and ignorance, in a dangerous world.

- **Implications:** children need the protection, guidance and instruction of adults—most importantly, their parents.

- Challenge parents not to shirk that responsibility.

5. Naturally wayward

- Point out the fact that no one has to teach a child to lie, to be mean or cruel. *(There are plenty of examples of waywardness in little children that you can give eg: grabbing the biggest cake, wanting a toy as soon as little brother has started to play with it.)*

- Contrast this tendency with the fact that parents have to work really hard to teach their children consideration for others eg: saying please and thank you, sharing toys, etc.

- Mention that the Bible calls this tendency 'sin', and that it is a regrettable part of every one of us—even parents!

- **Implications:** We should not be shocked or even mildly surprised when our children behave like this.

6. A blank sheet of paper

- Explain that this view stresses the effects that parents will have on their children. People believe *everything* that parents do and don't do has long-term consequences for their child.

- Give a couple of illustrations (there are many) eg: eating beetroot in pregnancy enhances your child's agility, or playing Bach improves a child's mathematical ability (point out that these examples are both fictional!)

- **Problem:** parents become paranoid. They exhaust themselves and spend a fortune to adjust every known variable to give their child the best chances.

- **Implications:** When children have problems, it is always the fault of the parents.

7. Genetically programmed

- Explain that this view holds that everything about us is caused by our genes, so the influence of parents counts for little or nothing.

- **Problem:** people can't and don't live consistently with this view. Most would accept that our genes determine our gender, the colour of our eyes, our natural abilities, etc. But most would also believe that even the most gifted tennis player needs a coach.

- You could comment on the fact that we have a deep desire to control the destinies of our children. This is what fuels the endless nature/nurture debate—the attempt to sort out those things that are the result of our genes from those that are the result of influences like our parents. Shouldn't it be obvious that the development of a human being is far too complex to even attempt to separate out all the variables? Perhaps this desire to be so in control of our child's destiny is in itself an unhealthy mistake. Perhaps our child's destiny is best left to other, bigger hands. Which raises the question: *what then should a parent be doing?*—see point 8 below.

8. A gift from God

- This view sees each child as a unique personality with a range of potentials that we are responsible for nurturing. Parents can greatly affect whether this potential is realised or not. Be prepared to illustrate these two aspects of a child's development, if people are not yet entirely clear. *Eg: a child born with a gift for music may or may not become a great musician, depending on how much or how little his parents could encourage him and give him opportunities to learn an instrument etc.*

- Contrast this with the previous view of children with parents who regard even an unplanned baby as a precious gift from God. They feel both awe and trepidation at the task they are about to undertake.

- Point out that this is an idea found in the Bible, and brings a sane and helpful balance to the nature/nurture debate that has been illustrated by points 6 and 7 above.

- **Implication 1:** With great gifts come great responsibilities. The job of a parent is to shape the character, attitudes and gifts of their child. The way in which a parent sets their child's course in life will have far more impact on the future of this planet than what they do at work, or how much they recycle their waste. This has more to do with the character and attitudes of you as parents than what you spend on them, or how much you invest in their education.

- **Implication 2:** If your child is a gift from God, it would be sensible to follow the Maker's instructions. *(You could give an illustration of disaster that occurred when you had neglected to read the instructions for a new gadget.)*

- Highlight the fact that God our Maker has given us written instructions—the Bible has practical and sound advice for parents, which has stood the test of time and experience and holds true for everybody, regardless of background or belief.

'An arrow into the future'

- This is a helpful image for understanding your role as a parent. You can never be sure that your child will 'turn out as you would like them to.' As they grow up, they will start to make their own decisions in life. But, in the same way that you take aim with an arrow, you will want to point your child in the right direction. The values and disciplines of life you teach them from an early age will help them enormously in the future.

- This is part of the **loving authority** that you exercise over your children. You can only exercise this properly when you understand that your child is a gift from God. It is not authority to make you feel good. It is authority you exercise so that they will grow and be nurtured in love.

- *End this part of the session by enthusing the parents; point out that parenting is an awesome responsibility, but also an exciting and enjoyable assignment.*

Break for refreshments (5 minutes) or end Session 1 here, reminding people of what is coming next week, and pointing them to the discussion questions on page 11 of the Study Guide.

Group Discussion 2: (10 minutes maximum)

See page 11 of the Study Guide. The purpose of this discussion is to help people understand that there are different ways of parenting (some clearly better than others), to think about what their own style of parenting is, and why that might be (are they reflecting or reacting against their own upbringing?). Some of the parents on your course may have experienced an abusive or neglectful upbringing; as course leader, you will need to be prepared to respond appropriately to people who reveal painful, personal issues. However, it is important to stress that this session focuses on the mistakes of well-meaning and loving parents, rather than abusive or neglectful ones.

Presentation B: Parenting pitfalls? (20-30 minutes)

The purpose of this presentation is to expose the kinds of mistakes in parenting that are commonly made by mostly well-intentioned and loving, but imperfect parents. The overall point made is that many of the problems of parenting are due to the parents, rather than the children. The presentation gives practical antidotes to these ineffective and counter-productive habits. These antidotes reflect the importance of the three principles on which the rest of the course focuses, and which will be introduced next session—relationship, communication and discipline.

• •

Gospel opportunity: There are a number of points in this presentation where the teaching of the Bible can be mentioned. For instance:

A is for Allow anything: the Bible teaches that parents have God-given authority over their child eg: the fifth commandment.

B is for Bribery: children, like all of us, are moral beings and are capable of making moral choices, although the extent of this will vary with age. This fits with what the Bible teaches about what God expects from people (eg: Romans 1 v 18-20, 2 v 12-16).

E is for Explosive: the Bible teaches that a key characteristic of a wise person is self-control (see Proverbs).

G is for Guilty: the answer to real guilt is forgiveness from the appropriate person; perhaps this means asking your child for forgiveness, just as the Bible instructs all of us to seek forgiveness from God.

It's not necessary to always make all these points, nor to spend a lot of time elaborating on them. A sprinkling of 'throw-away' comments to entice and intrigue people is probably the best approach.

• •

27

Outline of Presentation B:

Introductory comments

- Introduce the central problem of parenting—you can't get the staff! Point out that none of us has a super-parent hidden inside of us, simply waiting for us to find the key that will let them out.

- Point out that most parenting is based on an assortment of ideas from various sources—some of them conflicting. None of us is an expert.

- Highlight the fact that even when we know the best way to proceed, we don't always follow it— we also have to battle with our own lack of patience, bad temper, selfishness etc. In fact, we suffer from the same 'disease' as our children.

- Emphasise that the problem with parenting is *NOT* that we don't love our children. Rather, in order to cope with our children, we get into habits (because of unhelpful ideas or our own weakness and failures) that make the problems worse or cause new ones.

- Refer to p11 of Study Guide. Introduce the 'Alphabet of Parenting Pitfalls', listed in the grid. (Reassure people that the list doesn't go all the way to Z!). Stress the fact that these are things we do as loving parents, not necessarily as unloving ones.

1. A is for Allow anything

- **The problem:** Parents don't believe that they have the right to insist on certain things from their children.

- **Illustration:** If you have none of your own, use the following:

  A parent finds it really hard to force her four-year-old to wear a seatbelt. They have a fight every time they get in the car. But, why is not wearing a seat-belt ever an option? How does the fact that the four-year-old doesn't like it make any difference to anything? The law is the law.

  GPs and practice nurses report a huge problem in giving immunisation injections, because the parent is afraid to insist that the child sits still on his/her mother's lap. The child runs and hides under the table and the parent says: 'She doesn't like needles... perhaps we'll try another day.'

- **Reasons:**

  a. Parents worry about inhibiting self-expression or damaging a child's self-esteem if they insist on things that children don't like.

  b. Parents are unwilling to confront their children because it is unpleasant. Rather, they have picked up from somewhere the (wrong) idea that it is important to be positive and encouraging all the time.

  c. Parents give in to their children because they are tired or feel lazy. Confrontation is hard work.

  d. Parents are afraid that their children won't love them.

- **Result:** The result of an 'allow anything' long-term strategy is an anxious child, who is badly behaved and generally unhappy.

- **Antidote:** Point out that parents have a responsibility to protect the vulnerable, direct the lost, correct the wayward and instruct the ignorant. (Mention the fact that the Bible teaches that parents have God-given authority over their children, and we also find that God Himself is the best model of loving parental authority.)

Challenge the parents to love their children enough to correct and insist, and encourage them to be confident that they not only have the right, but also the responsibility to exercise loving authority over their children.

2. B is for Bribery

- **The problem:** Parents try to change the behaviour of their child, or persuade them to do better by offering them rewards. Or by threatening sanctions.

- **Illustration:** If you have none of your own, use the following:
  Following the publication of a long-awaited Harry Potter sequel, the Daily Telegraph carried a Matt cartoon, showing a weary parent trying to get a contrary child to go to bed. It showed the parent holding a Harry Potter book over the fire and saying to the horrified child: 'Go to bed or Harry Potter gets it!'

- **Reasons:**

    a. In the short-term bribery can be extremely effective.

    b. Reward systems are highly recommended in some circles eg: trouble-shooting parenting programmes on television (but these tend to deal with extreme cases where discipline has gone badly wrong, so here, bribery constitutes damage-limitation rather than an effective long-term strategy for controlling children.

- **Result:** Reward systems do not produce self-discipline and self-motivation. They have an outward effect but they do not produce inner qualities like kindness or consideration. A child learns to produce just enough to earn the reward, but not to love good behaviour for its own sake. The result of the bribery strategy is actually *an unmotivated child,* who is denied the discovery of the pleasure of doing things for their own sake, and who thinks that behaviour is negotiable.

- **Antidote:** Explain that it is better to base your behaviour management on your relationship with your child, and make sure that your standards for their behaviour are rooted in ideas of what is right and wrong. *(Give an illustration of how this would work eg: A child should be encouraged to tidy up their toys because it helps the whole family to enjoy living in a tidy house, and it is kind to mum, who has a lot of other things to do.)*

- Point out that children are moral beings capable of making moral choices.

- Encourage parents not to ignore this inbuilt 'friend', in seeking to instil good patterns of behaviour in their child.

- Challenge the parents to love their child enough to take the long-term view.

3. C is for Child-centred

- **The problem:** Parents organise their lives so that everything is right for the children.

- **Illustration:** If you have none of your own, use the following:
  A common sight in some parts of the country is the mother at the wheel of her 4WD vehicle, with two or more pampered offspring strapped in the back, going from ballet to brownies to riding to friend's sleepover. Every evening, every weekend, it is the same: a full programme of activities to entertain or educate the children.

- **Reasons:**

  a. You want to be the perfect parent.

  b. It's a habit that people pick up when they bring their first baby home; their life is turned upside-down, and everything revolves around that delightful but demanding infant and its routines (or lack of them!).

- **Result:** Explain that the child-centred approach to parenting gives your child the mistaken idea that he or she is the centre of the universe, which is definitely not the case. You are raising a brat. The result of this is a helpless and selfish child who expects to be entertained and victimises the whole family.

- Such continual slavery to the needs of the children is extremely unhealthy for the parents, for their relationship together, and all the family.

- **Antidote:** Encourage the parents to organise their family life so that they are not the slave or victim of any one member. Challenge them to love their child enough to safeguard against making them the centre of your life.

4. D is for Distant

- **The problem:** The distant parent is a parent taken up with other things—work, career, another relationship, a hobby, etc.

- **Illustration:** If you have none of your own, use the following:
  In Dickens' 'Bleak House', there is a character called Mrs Jellyby, who apparently has a huge heart for people a long way off (the orphans of Borrioboola-Ga), but ignores or is unaware of the fact that her own children are tumbling up and down the stairs, in a state of appalling neglect.

31

- **Reasons:**

  a. Distant parents perhaps have had poor relationships with their own parents and are thus afraid to get too close to their children.

  b. A distant parent can be one who is so obsessed by the desired end-product for the child, that they forget that there is a real person in there. Parenting becomes all about getting the best education and opportunities, working long hours to achieve these goals. No time is left to just relax with the child and enjoy his or her company for its own sake.

- **Result:** The result of distant parenting is an angry child.

- **Antidote:** Challenge parents to love their child enough to get involved with them.

5. E is for Explosive

- **The problem:** Parents only react when a child's behaviour reaches a level of irritation or unacceptability that the parent finds unbearable. They then react by losing their temper—shouting, hitting, dishing out severe penalties, cutting the child down with a sarcastic or cruel remark, etc.

- **Illustration:** If you have none of your own, use the following:
  Picture the scene—the children are playing and it turns to bickering and squabbling. The temperature is rising. Suddenly someone screeches and it gets to you and you boil over. You go ballistic. Children are separated, shouted at, spanked, sent to their rooms; heavy-duty extreme sanctions are imposed. In such a case you have been reactive, not proactive.

- **Reasons:**

  a. Being explosive can apparently be very effective in the short-term.

  b. On the other hand, being proactive—taking steps earlier to make sure that unacceptable behaviour doesn't happen—takes a lot more time, energy and involvement from the parent.

- **Result:**

  a. Warn parents that being explosive with your child may lead you to do something you will really regret.

  b. The result of using explosive behaviour to control your children is a child who has learned he can carry on until there is a scene. Only at a certain decibel level will the switch be triggered to modify his behaviour. This is a very long way from the desired result: a self-disciplined child.

c. An 'exploding' parent will teach their child very negative ways of handling frustration.

- **Antidote:** Encourage the parents to be a thermostat, rather than a thermometer, by being proactive in a situation where the temperature is rising. Divert, distract, correct or remove. Do not explode.

- Many parents hit their children when they are reacting explosively. Encourage the parents to spot the danger signals in themselves and, if they are angry, to put their hands behind their back and keep them there.

You may wish to point out that this course deals with the smacking issue in the next session. At this point, simply stress that smacking should never be about dealing with your own anger.

6. F is for Fault-finding

- **The problem:** This is more than simply being conscientious about correcting a child. Correction is one thing, but a continual stream of disparaging comments is another, especially when it has an unmistakable flavour of 'Why can't you be more like Miranda?' *Note that putting a child down may be seen as a joke or a tease by a parent, but inasmuch as it rubbishes the child's efforts, it can be extremely damaging.*

- **Illustration:** (Your illustration)

- **Reasons:** Parents can become like this if they are always comparing their child with other people's children. These parents care about the child's achievements or behaviour because they want to impress other parents. We all enjoy a bit of reflected glory and we can be envious of others whose children always seem to be on top form.

- **Result:** The result of the fault-finding habit is a discouraged child, who lacks confidence.

- **Antidote:** Challenge the parents to recognise the efforts of their child, to look for opportunities to give genuine encouragement and to love them for who they are.

7. G is for Guilty.

- **The problem:** Guilt may be real, false or imagined.

  a. **False guilt**—where parents feel guilty for things beyond their control. Perhaps you are on a low income; perhaps you are a lone parent. These situations may well have an adverse effect on a child, but parents also tend to overstate these negative effects.

  b. **Imaginary guilt**—where parents sometimes suffer a continual sense of inadequacy, as though they could never be quite good enough, provide enough, prevent enough.

  c. **Real guilt**—where you have behaved in a mean or unworthy manner towards your child. That needs to be faced honestly and squarely, and dealt with.

- Whatever the source of the guilt, the parent needs to beware of seeking to make up for the problem inappropriately.

- **Illustration:** If you have none of your own, use the following:

  It has been noticed that less well-off or single parents spend a far greater proportion of their income on their children's clothes and toys. It is the middle classes who tend to make use of charity shops, jumble sales and hand-me downs. Other parents, whose guilt is to do with a consciousness of neglect, may try and make up for it by buying expensive toys.

- **Reasons:**

  a. **False and imaginary guilt**—failure to understand or accept that we cannot be perfect parents or what makes a good parent.

  b. **Real guilt**—failure to seek or accept forgiveness for what we have done wrong.

- **Result:** The result of guilty parenting will be a manipulative child, one who learns how to use victim status, one who will blame you.

- **Antidote:**

  a. **False guilt**—encourage parents to focus on those things that are most important for their child, and within their capability to provide, such as the quality of their relationship, healthy values, precious memories, etc.

  b. **Imaginary guilt**—reassure parents that God does not expect them to be perfect, but merely responsible.

34

c. Real guilt—point out that the answer to real guilt is forgiveness, from the appropriate person – perhaps from the child, perhaps from God. Encourage parents to get these matters sorted out as soon as possible, preferably on the same day. Challenge them to develop an atmosphere in their home which says we are all sinners. Reassure them that children are very forgiving and, strangely enough, so is God.

8. H is for Hedging

- **The problem:** This describes parents who surround and limit their children for their own safety because the world is a dangerous place, or for the sake of a quiet life because they know their child's capacity for naughtiness.

- **Illustrations:** If you have none of your own, use the following:

  'I was walking in the park last autumn and noticed on the ground hundreds of beautiful shiny brown conkers. 'What is this?' I thought to myself. 'Why are these conkers not filling children's pockets and being baked or soaked in vinegar and then threaded on strings, for hours of fun in the street or playground?' Well, one reason is that children are kept too much indoors or engaged in adult-organised, adult-supervised activities. Not only are they not joyfully roaming the parks, they are not playing in the street, because parents perceive that as too risky. Sad, sad days we live in!'

- **Reasons:**

  a. These parents may overwhelmingly regard the world as a dangerous place from which it is their responsibility to protect their children.

  b. Or, for the sake of a quiet life, these parents want to avoid any scope for misbehaviour.

- **Result:** The result of too much hedging is a deceitful child, who will not manage independence well. They think it is your job to manage their behaviour.

- **Antidote:** Encourage the parents to build in opportunities for independence, as their children grow. They should allow them the freedom to fail, even sometimes to get hurt, because this is how they learn. Challenge the parents to love them enough to let them go.

9. I is for Inconsistency

- **The problem:** This describes parents who issue threats that they never carry out, or who only attempt to enforce standards of behaviour when others are present. Children learn that adults say all sorts of things that are just noise and bluster, so they don't have to take much notice. *Point out that this could be the most serious pitfall of all.*

- **Illustration:** If you have none of your own, use the following:
  You go to collect your child from a friend's house, where he has been to play and to have tea. On the doorstep, among the goodbyes, you whisper to your child to say 'thank you for having me' to the child's mother, who is standing there smiling benignly. Your child goes all tight-lipped and obstinate. So you whisper more menacingly into his ear. No response. You are embarrassed in front of your friend (whose child always has wonderful manners); you are also livid and, on the way home, you threaten extreme penalties. But the trouble is that you have not been consistently insisting that your child says 'thank you' at other times when nobody's mother is watching.

  Sometimes you hear a hassled mother scream at her child as they struggle down the high street: 'Do that once more, and I'll kill you.' You know, or you hope you know, that the mother does not mean it. The child also knows it, which is why this sort of attempt at discipline is so ineffective.

- **Reasons:**

  a. **Thoughtlessness**—parents say things that they don't mean.

  b. **Parents may be more interested in the effects of their child's behaviour on themselves than in the behaviour itself.** They intervene only when the child's behaviour is embarrassing or irritating them— otherwise they let it pass.

  c. **Laziness or weariness**—consistent parenting is hard work; parents must be constantly alert to what their children are doing, and always ready to intervene and carry out what they have said.

- **Result:** The result of inconsistent parenting is an unruly child, who becomes progressively harder to control.

- **Antidote:** Encourage the parents to promise only what they intend to deliver, and then to deliver as promised. Challenge them to love their children enough to say what they mean and follow it through.

SUMMARY OF THIS SESSION

- Point out that the trouble with parenting is usually the parent, so the key to tackling many parenting problems is not with the child but with the parent, who might need to recognise some areas for change himself or herself. The bad news about parenting is that there are no perfect parents.

- Reassure people that this session is not meant to discourage them, but that by understanding the common pitfalls of parenting they can avoid falling into them or at least doing so repeatedly.

- Emphasise that no one has to be a super-parent (a perfect parent) to be an effective one. While your love for your child may lead you into some of the above pitfalls, it is also true to say that love (ordinary affection and tenderness) covers a multitude of sins, and that most mistakes can be corrected.

End by highlighting the good news of this session—that imperfect parents can raise delightful human beings, provided they are not afraid to grasp God–given authority and be parents.

Group Discussion 3 (10 minutes maximum)

Refer to p13 of Study Guide and introduce the discussion questions.

- Point out that these questions will help the group to summarise what they have learned this session.

Closing comments (5 minutes maximum)

Refer to p14 of Study Guide and draw attention to the **Think through at home** questions. These are for people to think about at home (preferably both parents together) before the next session. Note that there are no right or wrong answers.

Introduce the subject of the next session: Discipline—the Big D-word. This is the reason why most people sign up for parenting courses.

2: THE BIG D-WORD—DISCIPLINE!

Please read these notes ahead of time and use them to ensure that you are well-prepared for leading the session.

Key concept:
Loving obedience

Theological basis:
God's ways are best for everybody. His commandments are the most liberating, healthiest, happiest way to live. Human beings are responsible and accountable for their actions.

Gospel opportunity:
God wants a relationship with us. We back off because we know we are guilty. Sin must be punished but God has sent Jesus to pay for our sins so that we can be restored to a relationship with God.

Preparing for Session 2
- **Evaluation:** Review the previous session and think about how effective it was.
  - *Did people seem happy and comfortable?*
  - *Did people seem to understand what was taught?*
  - *Was the room well-organised? If not, what changes should be made?*
  - *Were the right kind of refreshments available?*

- *Did the session run according to schedule? If not, what were the problems? Eg: Did the break take longer than expected? Did people take up time with questions? Did the presentations go on too long?*

- *Were you able to make use of any gospel opportunities?*

- **Resources:** It may be helpful to have a whiteboard or flipchart and marker pens available during this session. This can be used for showing words that some parents may have problems spelling eg: 'authoritative', 'authoritarian' and 'permissive'. It can also be used to show people how to complete the 'magic triad' diagram on p16 of the Study Guide.

  - Make sure you have a few extra copies of Study Guides in case of further newcomers, or people who have forgotten to bring their copy to the session.

- **Assistance:** Check that you have organised people to help with welcoming and refreshments.

- **Film extract:** If you are using a film clip, make sure that the extract is set up for viewing, and that curtains or blinds can quickly be drawn, or are already closed at the beginning of the session.

Introduction and time to settle down	*5 minutes*
Film extract and discussion	*10 minutes*
Presentation C—*includes a group activity*	*20-30 minutes*
Group discussion 2	*10 minutes*
Refreshments and toilet break	*5 minutes*
Presentation D	*20-30 minutes*
Group discussion 3	*10 minutes*
Wrap up	*5 minutes*
Total	**1 hour 45 minutes**

C: Communication

- To build on what has been established in Session 1; namely, that it is right and good for parents to exercise loving authority over their children. Remind your group that children are vulnerable both because of their innocence of the world around, and because of their waywardness.

- To examine what it means to be authoritative, rather than authoritarian or permissive, and to encourage parents to be authoritative (See Film extract and Group discussion 1: p15 of Study Guide).

- To introduce the 'magic triad' of three interdependent aspects of parenting—communication, discipline and relationship—that are all equally important in the task of raising children well (See p16 of Study Guide).

- To focus on communication and discipline, and examine what is involved in each of these.

- To examine and teach more skilful ways of speaking and listening to children (see p17of Study Guide).

- To talk about why and how parents should encourage their children's language skills development.

D: Discipline

- To explain what discipline is.

- To examine reasons why children misbehave and how parents can respond appropriately (see Presentation D: p19 of Study Guide)..

- To teach a three-fold strategy for effective discipline (see p20-21 of Study Guide).

Introduction and settle down (5 minutes maximum)

Allow 5 minutes for people to settle down, to run through everyone's names if you wish and to check that everyone has a copy of the Study Guide. Make sure people have name labels.

- Give a brief overview of what you will do in the session, and move quickly on to the film extract.

Film extract (10 minutes maximum with the discussion)

*Refer to p15 of Study Guide and point out the questions to be answered after viewing the extract. Introduce the extract from **The Sound of Music**, with a brief summary of how Maria has come to be in the position of governess to seven motherless children, and asking people to look out for the differences between the father and Maria with regard to raising children. The purpose of the film extract is to show an example of an authoritarian approach to parenting (in Captain Von Trapp), and to give an opportunity to discuss, not only the problems of this style of parenting, but also the alternative (as suggested by Maria). This will be preparatory to an explanation of three styles of parenting—authoritarian, permissive, and authoritative—in which being authoritative is described and commended as the best approach.*

> **The extract:** After a time of absence Captain Von Trapp returns home accompanied by the woman whom he hopes to make his new wife. He is somewhat embarrassed and annoyed when his children and Maria make a riotous entrance. They are dressed in 'play-clothes', which Maria has made out of old curtains; they have been climbing trees and playing in the river; they are wet, noisy and apparently disorganised. The Captain blows his whistle to restore order and tells Maria that she has let the children become wild. Maria for her part accuses the Captain of not even knowing his children.

Group discussion 1

Talk around your tables about this film. Let those who have seen the whole film describe to the others Captain Von Trapp's style of parenting.

Presentation C: Communication (20-30 minutes)

This presentation begins with a review of Session 1, to remind parents of their God-given responsibility to exercise loving authority over their children.

Three styles of parenting are then mentioned; two that are inadequate—authoritarian and permissive parenting—and one that is commended—authoritative parenting. To demonstrate what is involved in being an authoritative, rather than authoritarian parent, reference is made to the 'magic triad' of three interdependent aspects of parenting—communication, discipline and relationship— all of which are equally important in the task of raising children well. This presentation focuses on communication.

The presentation examines four stages of what is involved in communication between a parent and child. Obstacles to good communication are identified, and ways of improving both listening and speaking are examined.

• •

Gospel opportunity: The conclusion that authoritative parenting is best (as opposed to authoritarian or permissive parenting) is not just a matter of common sense. This is exactly what Christians see in God.

The God of the Bible is never distant and uninvolved in the world He has made. On the contrary, the Bible itself has resulted from God's constant communication with humans throughout history. God's greatest grief is that people don't want any sort of relationship with him (Romans 1 v 18-23). But God has also acted in history to restore the relationship of trust and dependence on Him that people had at the beginning of creation. God again becomes the perfect heavenly Father of those who trust in Him. We are told: 'As a father has compassion on his children, so the Lord has compassion on those who fear him;' (Psalm 103 v 13). But the Bible teaches clearly that God must punish wrong-doing. We are also told that God disciplines those he loves (Hebrews 12 v 5-11), in a passage that also commends discipline by human parents. God is equally committed to both punishing wrong-doing and making it possible for people who do wrong to enjoy a loving relationship with him—this explains his purpose in sending Jesus Christ to die on a cross. The 'magic triad' features of relationship, communication and discipline are all found in God.

43

As the fatherhood of God is something unique to Christianity, it may be a new idea to people in your group that in Christ we can relate to God as our perfect heavenly Father. If people are intrigued by or attracted to the fatherhood of God, the next question to lead people to think about is: Who are given the right to become children of God? The answer, found in John 1 v 12-13, is those who receive Jesus and believe in His name.

•••

Outline of Presentation C

Introductory comments

- Recap Session 1

- Remind people that a loving parent is one that takes responsibility for their child. Your child is…

    uniquely created

    a gift from God

    innocent—and therefore vulnerable because of their ignorance

    yet also **wayward**—and therefore in need of boundaries

    and **an arrow into the future**—which means that your influence as a parent is key in setting the direction of your child's life.

- Remind people that a loving parent loves their child enough to…

    exercise authority over them

    take the long-term view of what is good and helpful

    safeguard against letting their child believe they are the centre of the universe

    let them go when appropriate

    always deliver what they promise and only promise
    what they intend to deliver.

- Remind the group of the key concept from Session 1—**loving authority.**

1. Three styles of parenting

Refer to p16 of Study Guide and point out the questions on styles of parenting.

- Summarise the Captain's view of child–rearing: children need more discipline; parents give orders and expect them to be obeyed; he is **authoritarian** (write this word on a board or flip chart for people to copy if necessary).

- Mention how this kind of parenting produces angry and deceitful children.

- Explain that many parents, in an attempt to avoid being authoritarian, fall into the opposite trap of being **permissive** (write this word on a board or flip chart for people to copy if necessary).

- Describe a parent who is permissive—someone who avoids, or is incapable of setting and enforcing any limits at all on their children's behaviour.

- Mention how this kind of parenting produces undisciplined, badly-behaved children.

- Challenge the parents to take seriously their responsibility for the social and moral upbringing of their child/children.

- Explain that the antidote to authoritarian parenting is not to be permissive but **authoritative** (write this word on the board if necessary).

- Describe a parent who is authoritative (rather than authoritarian): someone who... has firm views about behaviour; gives clear and consistent messages about right and wrong; encourages good behaviour and discourages bad behaviour; is not a bully.

- Contrast Maria's understanding of the children with that of the Captain: her view was that they needed more love and a closer relationship with their father. The issue is not just about how many or few rules should be strictly enforced.

2. How to be authoritative, not authoritarian

- Introduce the topic of Session 2—discipline.

- Point out that it's tempting to think of discipline as something in isolation, rather like setting up a system, but that's not so (as we have just seen in *The Sound of Music*).

- Remind everyone that the Captain had to learn that discipline was only effective in the context of a warm relationship—it is not enough to be strict.

- Introduce the saying: *Rules without relationship lead to rebellion*.

- Tell your group about the 'magic triad'—three things, none of which work without the other two. All three are crucial if you are aiming to raise a delightful human being:

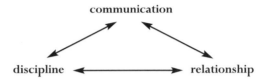

- Refer to p16 of the Study Guide, where these three words are printed. Ask the parents to draw lines to join the words in a triangle, with one of the three words at each angle of the triangle. Then, on each side of the triangle, ask them to draw arrow-heads at each end of the line, pointing in opposite directions. (Show an example on whiteboard/flipchart.)

- Explain that discipline, relationship and communication belong together—as each one of these improves, it enhances the other two.

- **Communication**   - improves the relationship

                              - improves discipline, since you and your child are better able to listen to each other

- **Good discipline**   - improves your relationship because you are more free to enjoy the company of your child

                              - enhances communication because you understand each other better

- **A good relationship** - improves communication because you know each other better

                              - improves discipline because it is the only effective setting for it

3. Communication

Refer to p16 of the Study Guide and introduce the four things that need to happen in order for communication to take place:

- parent speaks
- child listens
- child speaks
- parent listens

- Point out that these things don't happen automatically. Each is a skill which has to be learned, and can always be improved.

- You can describe the process of communication as follows:

  a. You have something in your mind, which you want to communicate to your child.

  b. You must decide what words, tone of voice and body posture you will adopt as you speak.

  c. You must think about whether your child is listening and understands or interprets those words in the way that you intend. *(The same things apply when your child wants to communicate something to you.)*

- List some of the things that can get in the way of good communication:
  - **Distractions**—other things that are happening around you
  - **Limited vocabulary**—not knowing or finding the right words
  - **Unclear speech**
  - **Inability to understand** what is being said
  - **Thinking about something else** when someone is talking to you etc.

Speaking: *tone of voice*

- **Illustration:** Tone of voice is something even a young baby with minimal grasp of language can understand. That is why we use a gentle soothing tone to calm a baby – it is not the words that they understand when they stop crying. On the other hand, it is easy to make a baby cry by adopting a harsh tone of voice. It doesn't actually matter what you are saying.

- Ask the group to find different ways of saying a word like 'sorry', simply by changing the tone of voice. Point out that it can mean almost the opposite of its standard meaning with certain tones of voice.

- **Speaking:** *body language*

    Group activity: Ask the group to make the following statements, without using words:

    'What you have to say is unimportant.'
    'That is inappropriate behaviour.'
    'You are very special.'

- Remind parents that these are skills that we can all improve. This means that parents need to make a priority of encouraging clear speech and developing language skills in their children.

- Highlight the importance of spending time talking and listening to your child, making all kinds of conversation—facts, opinions, feelings and fantasy—an important part of daily life in your home.

- Warn parents about the dangers of too much television. Although there is a lot of language on television, children do not learn to communicate well by watching it. Rather, the evidence suggests that children who watch a lot of television have a smaller vocabulary and less-developed language skills.

- **Listening:** *the need for interpretation*

    - Emphasise that speaking is only half the story; learning to listen is harder.

    - **Illustration:** *If you have none of your own, use the following:*
    When our children are first learning to talk and we, the enthralled and devoted parent, are amazed at the genius in our midst, we get used to trying to interpret. 'Dink!' he shouts and we say: 'Oh, you want a drink.' 'Lollo!' – 'Yes, that's a lorry, it's a red lorry.' That is how children learn English. The natural reaction of repeating back continues to be an effective tool in communication even when their vocabulary is apparently as large as yours. It is a way of checking that they mean what you think they mean.

- Point out that as our children grow older, we still need to interpret the words that they speak to us if we are to be effective at listening to them. This is because the true meaning of what our child is saying can be masked by the actual words used.

- **Group activity:** Ask your group what they understand by the following statements, and how they would respond:

  'I'm hopeless at reading.' (an expression of discouragement—not an invitation to discuss literacy skills)

  'It's not fair. I never get treats.' (this child feels cheated or overlooked—they don't want a list of all previous occasions when they have received treats, proving the statement wrong, but rather, reassurance and sympathy)

  'My team won at games today.' (an expression of pleasure—not just a statement of fact—and an invitation for you to share their pleasure)

  'I'm not playing with Katie any more.' (again, not a statement of fact but an expression of hurt, looking for an appropriate response)

- Summarise by pointing out how we can often be too literal in our response— taking the words at face value, instead of listening and responding to the heart message that lies behind the words.

Listening: *teaching children the skill of listening*

- Mention the fact that, in the age of television, children are entering the school system with increasingly poor listening skills—ask any reception class teacher.

- **Illustration:** *If you have none of your own use the following:*
  Observe a reception class sitting on the carpet with their teacher. The teacher gives an instruction in words. Roughly a third of the children will hear, decode and follow the instruction (eg: 'Fetch your writing book and a pencil). Another third will not hear and decode, yet seconds later they are complying with the instruction. How did they do that, without listening? They have learnt the skill of watching what other children do and copying what they are doing. The other third will not be even aware of the instruction nor of the activity of the other children because they do not understand even what instructions are for; they think they are just so much background noise to their lives. So approximately two thirds of four-year-olds are poor or very poor at listening.

- Explain that teaching to listen gets much harder as children grow older, since, by the age of four, many have become habitual non-listeners.

- Give some examples of enjoyable ways to teach young children to listen

  - Games like 'Simon says'

  - Reading stories together

  - Telling a story, as opposed to reading one. This can be a well-known fairy tale. Use eye-to-eye contact. This can be like saying 'Come and play with me', as together you enter a world where words conjure up pictures in the mind.

  - Instructions—give instructions (without the visual aid of you showing them) and see if your child can decode them. As your child grows, practise giving two or three instructions at once.

  - Instructions game—you and your child give multiple bizarre instructions and see if you can remember them. Eg:

    Put a cushion on your head.

    Stand on one leg with a cushion on your head.

    Stick your finger in your ear, stand on one leg with a cushion on your head.

    Fetch a spoon, stick your finger in your ear, stand on one leg with a cushion on your head.

- End this part of Session 2 by pointing out that listening is an invaluable life skill, which only parents can teach. Remind people that the most important preparation for school is the ability to listen. The child who cannot listen, cannot learn—whereas the child who can listen has a great advantage, whatever their natural ability.

Group discussion 2 (10 minutes maximum)

- Parents should talk about the following statements (refer to p18 of Study Guide), and try to improve on them by making them more personal, more specific or more encouraging.

  'That's absolutely wonderful.'

  'Look at Sarah's work. Can't you be a bit more like her?'

  'I'll find your book when I've finished making your sandwiches.'

  'Don't you dare play the recorder while I'm watching the news.'

  'Look at this mess. Do you have to be so clumsy?'

  'That's four words you didn't know on this page. You'll have to work harder at reading.'

- Each person can share childhood memories of something said that made either a positive or negative lasting impression.

Break for refreshments (5 minutes) or end here if you are doing a 6-session version of this course.

Presentation D: Discipline (45 minutes maximum)

Outline of Presentation D
Introductory comments

- Begin by pointing out that discipline is not the same as punishment; it involves far more.

- Explain that discipline is a system of training which includes:
  - instruction
  - correction
  - encouragement
  - modelling—leading by example
  - punishment—where necessary (which it will be!)

- Mention that children misbehave for a number of different reasons. Outline how important it is for a parent to first understand why their child is misbehaving, in order to decide what kind of discipline is required—should I punish my child in this situation or would it be better to correct them? Or do they not even know that they are doing something wrong? In which case, instruction is what is needed.

1. WHY DO CHILDREN MISBEHAVE?
Refer to p19 of Study Guide. Draw attention to the grid under the heading Why do children misbehave? People will need to fill this in as they listen to the presentation.

- Tell your group that misbehaviour can be due to any one or a combination of the following five main reasons.

a) to get attention
Illustration: *If you have none of your own, use the following:*
Imagine a toddler who finds his mother too taken up with attending to the needs of a new-born sister or brother. What does he do? He plays with the remote control or chucks his toys about the room or climbs on top of the cupboard. Any attention from Mum is better than no attention. **'Elliot, get down from that cupboard, this minute!'** *will do.*

- **Antidote:** Point out that the answer to this problem is to catch your child being good. Make sure your child gets plenty of attention and praise for doing the right thing. This is excellent training because it strengthens your relationship with the child, while you are explicitly stating what kind of behaviour or attitude meets your approval.

- **Illustration:** *A primary school class is bobbing about on the carpet, 90% of them paying absolutely no attention to the teacher. Does she shout:* **Wayne, sit still. Ryan, stop doing that. Georgina, be quiet!** *Not if she has any wisdom. Instead she says:* **Well done, Emma. You are sitting beautifully.** *Instantly, the rest of the class are curious to see what Emma is doing to get such a warm response from the only adult in the room. And the next minute, 30 six-year-olds have their arms folded, giving their undivided attention to the teacher. All done without shouting or tears!*

- Mention that behaviour management experts estimate that praise should outnumber correction by a ratio of 3:1, in order to encourage good behaviour.

b) to challenge authority

- **Illustration:** *If you have none of your own, use the following.*
  You have made it clear that your child is not to jump in a puddle but the child, with a cheeky glance over her shoulder, does it anyway. This is a test for you. Do you really mean what you say? Are you in charge or not?

- Emphasise that it is most important with this kind of misbehaviour to respond clearly and firmly.

- **Antidote:** Set boundaries and do not budge. Do not mind seeming grim. Do not fear the child's displeasure. It does not matter if Sarah-Jane goes to bed thinking Mummy and Daddy are harsh. She will get over it. What does matter is that Sarah-Jane goes to bed knowing who is in charge. Therein lies her security.

- Point out that a child's challenge to a parent's authority can also be shown in smaller ways. Tell the parents to watch out for attitude, as well as misbehaviour, and to pick up on the curled lip, the muttering under the breath, the cheeky answer.

c) to hurt

- **Illustration:** *If you have none of your own, use the following.*
  Imagine a child who has not been picked for the school football team. He comes out of school grumpy and tearful, but when his mum or dad tries to comfort him, he pushes them away, throws his bags on the ground and storms off. Misbehaviour can be an expression of anger. It is frequently against you precisely because they know that you will still love them.

53

- **Antidote:** Encourage the parents to continue to correct their child in this kind of situation, but to be gentle, since this is not a challenge to their authority.

  - Explain that they need to deal with the issue causing the anger, rather than the hurt to themselves.

  - Point out that sometimes this kind of misbehaviour brings out a quite childish and retaliatory streak in us: 'You've spoilt my day, so I'll spoil yours, sunbeam!' Warn the parents against retaliating in the same way.

  - Also warn them not to make excuses for the misbehaviour, at least, not in the child's hearing. Even though tiredness and frustration can be reasons for bad behaviour, they do not excuse it. Don't create a victim.

  - **Illustration:** *If you have none of your own, use the following.*
    Sometimes you will see even young children who have been playing up, but when they see coming wrath in the face of a parent, they quickly put down a trembling lip and whine: 'I'm tired.' They hope for the sympathy vote instead of the word of rebuke. They are already learning the power of victim status. Do not be taken in. Always stand by the message that we must all take responsibility for our behaviour, whatever the circumstances. But make a mental note to bring forward bedtime.

d) to win a friend's approval

  - **Illustration:** *If you have none of your own, use the following.*
    The author remembers her own two elder boys had a friend who enjoyed making mischief, and brought out in her sons a tendency to impress each other with acts of bravado. One afternoon, when they were playing quietly in the bedroom with this friend, she discovered them in the act of gleefully emptying every drawer, pulling the bed linen off the beds and the books off the shelves, in order to make a colossal mountain in the middle of the room. Each blamed the other two for egging him on.

  - Point out that we all adjust our behaviour and speech to the company we are in, because we want to be accepted.

  - **Antidote:** Training in behaviour must always be placed firmly in a moral framework. Teach your child that how they behave in any situation involves a moral choice, rather than following their feelings.

  - Teach them to ask themselves: Is it right or wrong to do this? Continually emphasise to your child that they can say 'no'!

- Remember that harmless mischief like demolishing a bedroom can be replaced in later years by more serious, or even criminal misbehaviour. Early training in making moral choices is the antidote to the peer-group pressure which is so strong during teenage years.

e) to signal inadequacy

- **Illustration:** *If you have none of your own, use the following:*
  1. Have you ever watched a young child with their parents in a posh restaurant? The child cannot cope with waiting for their food; they don't understand that in such a setting they should talk more quietly than they are allowed to at home. The child gets told off for fidgeting, being noisy and messing with the cutlery and cruet. The fact is that they are in the wrong place. Children misbehave when given inappropriate tasks to signal or to cover their inadequacy.

  2. In a classroom where there is a normal range of ability, if all the children are always given the same task, there will be times when those who are less able will muck about simply because they cannot do what is required of them. They are set up for failure – perhaps the task requires reading but they cannot read, so they play the clown instead. The wise teacher avoids this unnecessary situation by giving the children different and individually appropriate tasks that each one can at least reasonably attempt.

- **Antidote:** Encourage the parents to think ahead, if possible, about the situations that their child will be placed in, and to envisage how appropriate that situation will be for their particular child. Then they can take action to pre-empt any likely inappropriate behaviour.

- Point out that children sometimes misbehave when faced with too many choices. They can't decide, or they waver and change their minds, or they are unsettled and grumpy. A great virtue is made of choice in our society. But young children find choices complicated.

- **Illustration:** *One mother found breakfast was transformed by just having one kind of cereal on offer. Beware too many choices. Just Weetabix will do.*

- Conclude this section of the talk by highlighting the fact that, if a parent can identify the reason for their child's misbehaviour, they will know better how to respond appropriately.

2. THE PARENTS' RESPONSIBILITY

- Introduce this section of the talk by raising the next issue covered: how can a parent encourage good, and discourage bad behaviour?

- Refer to p20-21 of Study Guide, where people can take notes as they listen to the presentation.

A THREEFOLD STRATEGY
A: Expect Obedience
B: Decide on a particular focus
C: Turn a behaviour crisis into a learning opportunity

A: Expect obedience. *Draw attention to the key concept in Session 2: obedience (you can also remind people of the key concept of Session 1: loving authority).*

- Challenge the parents to think about cultivating a general expectation of obedience in their children.

- Remind your group of (or introduce them to) the fourth of God's Ten Commandments in the Bible: *'Honour your father and mother'*.

- **Effect on society:** get your group to think about the effect on our streets and in our schools if every family took this commandment seriously. Don't we all want to live in a society where children respect their parents, and where parents take responsibility in raising decent and upright citizens?

- **Effect on our children:** get your group to think about what following this commandment would do for their child's own protection and guidance. Is it not in our children's interest, and for their own safety, that they are taught to mind what their parents say, without challenge or delay?

- Point out that the time to work on this is with a toddler. Once it is grasped that obedience to you is essential for their safety and happiness, your discipline problems are over. Your child must do as you ask. It is not optional.

- **A training strategy:** *(Refer to p20 of Study Guide.)*

    1. Stop what you are doing and look at the child.

2. Wait until the child looks at you and stops. (That might mean getting down on the floor with them, so that you can be eyeball to eyeball.)

3. State what you want them to do, clearly, simply and once. If you repeat, children learn not to listen.

4. Ask the child what he is to do. If he doesn't know, say: 'Take a guess'.

5. Stand and wait (smiling). Resist the temptation to sit, slouch or tell off.

6. While standing and waiting, notice and mention everything your child does in the right direction.

- Point out that parents can expect this strategy to work. It takes time but it does not end in screaming.

- Stress the fact that parents need to give their undivided attention, rather than just giving an instruction and walking away.

- Encourage your group to expect that they will be rewarded with increased harmony in the home and an enhanced relationship with their child.

B: Decide on your particular focus

- Explain that parents will need to choose a focus for training at any one time, since we cannot cure all the bad habits of our children at once.

- Encourage people to choose one or two issues at most to concentrate on eg: table manners, behaviour at bedtime, putting away toys, sharing etc.

- Stress that parents need to think about the behaviour they want to see in their children, not just the behaviour they don't want.

- Emphasise the importance of partners agreeing on both the focus for training and the behaviour they want from their child, so that there will be absolute unanimity and consistency between the parents.

- *Refer to p20 of Study Guide so people can take notes as they listen.*

- **Establish the focus:** Parents should explain to the child how they want them to behave. They should talk with them about the particular thing that they want them to work on. For example:

  'This is how we are going to do bedtime from now on.'

'You need to learn how to look after your toys properly.'

- They should make sure the child understands what behaviour they are looking for, and avoid simply grumbling after the event. Remind people that sometimes children only discover a rule after they have broken it.

- Point out that parents need to be realistic when establishing the focus. They should bear in mind the age and maturity of their child, and choose a battle they can win. Small steps in the right direction are a triumph.

- **Explain the focus:** If appropriate, parents can ask their child why they should behave as the parent wants in the situation that has been chosen for the focus. Usually children can be made to see the benefits of good behaviour, even if it only means a quieter life for them!

- Reassure the parents that if their children can't see the point of behaving in the way that their parents would like, it is quite all right to say 'Because I say so'. Remind them that, as parents, their job is to protect the vulnerable, direct the lost and instruct the ignorant.

- Stress that it doesn't matter whether the child agrees or not—the most important thing is for the parent to be clear and fair.

- **Enact the focus:** Highlight the importance of being a role model. If the issue is grumbling, do you grumble? If it is untidiness, how tidy are you?

- Encourage the parents to draw attention to their own weakness in the particular area that they want changed. Suggest that if they openly try to change themselves as well, it can become a whole family project. For example:

  More tidiness in the home!

  It's thankfulness week!

- Remind your group to be inspiring and cheerful when showing their children how to behave well.

- **Enforce the focus:** Point out that it will do no good if everyone concentrates on the focus for a moment or too, only to forget about it half an hour later. (This is why it is good to focus on only a couple of things at a time.)

- Remind everyone that discipline includes **instruction, correction, modelling** and **encouragement**. They should use praise and encouragement as much as they can. They should also use patient correction. It is possible to correct without yelling—just say it.

- For example:

  'Remember what we said about moaning? Tell me something you can be grateful for.'
  'That is no way to leave your bedroom. What will you put away first?'

- Explain to your group that rebellion involves a challenge to their authority, and this is the point at which sanctions are needed.

Sanctions

- Mention that people can choose from three types of sanctions:
  - natural consequences
  - logical consequences
  - direct action

a. Natural consequences: Explain that these are the things that can happen as a result of misbehaviour.

- **Illustrations:** *If you have none of your own, use the following:*
  1. *The child who does not put his toys away will lose a vital part or, a precious toy will get stepped on and broken because it was left in the middle of the room. Do not rush to the toy shop to get a replacement. Natural consequences are your friend; do not protect your child from them.*

  2. *When your school-age child loses or neglects her homework, do not rush around to bale her out of trouble. And do not be annoyed with the teacher who gives her a detention. Shake that teacher by the hand and say: 'Thank you very much'. That teacher shares your aim of making your child responsible for her actions.*

b. Logical consequences: Point out that some misbehaviour suggests an obvious sanction.

- **Illustrations:** *If you have none of your own, use the following:*
  1. *The child who is later than the agreed time returning from a Saturday afternoon in town, is not allowed out the following Saturday.*

  2. *The child who shows off has to spend time alone in his bedroom.*

  3. *The child who grumbles misses a treat.*

c) **Direct action:** Point out that these are measures taken by a parent that are intentionally unpleasant for the child. They may include **'time out'**, **withdrawal of privileges** and **smacking**.

- Emphasise that direct action should follow certain principles:

- These sanctions should never occur when you are in a temper;

- The sanctions should follow promptly on the misbehaviour;

- They should be short;

- They should respect the child.

- Spend a few moments on the controversial subject of smacking. You could make some or all of the following points, which represent the author's view on smacking.

  - With young children, smacking has the advantage that it is immediate and easily understandable, and, in the author's experience, improves the relationship.

  - Smacking is most effective for children between the ages of eighteen months and four. In the author's experience, smacking was rarely, if ever, needed after that because the groundwork on discipline had been done, and the children had grasped the concept of obedience.

  - Smacking can be controversial, but usually only with parents who are squeamish and have a problem with the whole idea of authority, or who have baggage from their own relationships with violent or abusive parents.

  - Smacking does not automatically brutalise children—it should be a brief but clear expression, by a loving parent, that certain behaviour is unacceptable and must cease and not be repeated. It will, of course, be painful, but no punishment would be effective if it were not painful.

  - Is smacking responsible for the increase in violent behaviour in children? Perhaps this is the question that bothers us the most. But where is the evidence? For generations, parents have used corporal punishment to train and correct their children (admittedly, sometimes to excess). But only in the last two decades has there been this alarming rise in violence in children. In the same period, the confidence of parents to correct their children sensibly and reasonably, as they see fit, has been undermined. Draw your own conclusion.

- There are children for whom physical punishment would be neither necessary nor appropriate at any age. Some children respond immediately to a disapproving frown or a gentle rebuke. But many don't. Every child is different, so it is for each parent to decide about their own particular child, since they know their child better than anyone.

C: Turn a behaviour crisis into a learning opportunity.

- Remind parents that each time their child gets something wrong, the parent has an opportunity to teach. This is particularly helpful when parents feel concern at the number of times their child is misbehaving.

- Reassure your group that getting something wrong is not such a bad thing, because it shows an area of weakness or ignorance, which can now be improved.

- **Illustration:** *If you were to see a child's maths book in which every page was covered with ticks in red pen, you might think that the child was brilliant. But on closer examination and with more information, you might come to a completely different conclusion: this child isn't learning anything!*

- Introduce the following five questions that will help parents to turn a behaviour crisis into a learning opportunity and a positive experience. Stress that the five questions should be discussed...

    - alone with the child, following an incident of misbehaviour;

    - in a calm atmosphere where eye-contact is maintained.

A TEACHING STRATEGY

Refer to p21 of Study Guide so people can take notes as they listen.

- **Question 1: What did you do?** Children will always tell you what someone else did or what were the circumstances at the time. While those are not irrelevant, always bring them back to their own behaviour or response. This is the bit that they are responsible for.

- **Question 2: Was what you did the right or wrong thing to do?** Bring the discussion straight into the moral framework. If you are not angry and the situation is calm, the child will invariably admit that what he/she did was wrong.

- **Question 3: How might you have handled it in a better way?** The idea of this is to get the child to explore the different responses that were available to them. They need to be aware that there are always options. Be patient and let the child think of them, but you may have to help them out if they are really stuck.

- **Question 4: The next time a similar situation arises, what will you do?** The child can choose one of the options outlined in question 3. What you are looking for is a commitment to changed behaviour. This whole discussion has effectively become one of establishing a new focus (see p57-58 above).

- **Question 5: Now if a similar situation arises and you fail to deal with it in the way you have agreed, what do you think would be a fair punishment for not keeping your promise?** Both of you are now very clear about what the issue is, what you expect are and what sanctions will apply. You, the parent, have also been very kind; there has been no punishment this time, just a helpful problem-solving discussion.

- Warn parents to be meticulously careful in following up what they have discussed with their child. If they consistently carry out what they have said, their children may learn that when they misbehave and are then disciplined, it is a 'fair cop'. If they are not consistent, their children will learn that they do not need to remember or act on what has been discussed.

Summary of Session 2

a) The unrivalled partnership—truth and love

- Explain that in the Bible, truth and love go together eg: Christians are instruct-ed to speak 'the truth in love' (Ephesians 4 v 15). The Bible declares truth and love to be the essence of healthy communication. Without love you will crush your child; without truth you will smother him.

b) The ultimate product—self-correction

- **Illustration:** *When children are learning to sing, they get to a point where their ears tell them that they are singing a wrong note, so that they can move to the right one.*

- Point out that, as parents, we should want our children to take responsibility for their own actions, and to be motivated to change their behaviour to the right course of action, whatever the circumstances.

c) The unashamed propaganda—good children are happy children

- Draw attention to the well-known fact that badly-behaved children are always deeply unhappy. Reassure parents that it is not wrong to make this connection, because this is the way God made us. Encourage them to teach this to their chil-dren.

Group discussion 3 (10 minutes maximum)

Refer to p22 of Study Guide and introduce the group discussion questions. Point out that these questions will help the group to summarise what they have learned this ses-sion.

Closing comments (5 minutes maximum)

- Refer to p18 and 22 of Study Guide and draw attention to the **Think through at home** questions. These are for people to think about at home (preferably both parents together) before the next session. Note that there are no right or wrong answers.

- Introduce the subject of the next session, which is the third part of the 'magic triad'—relationship. Explain that you will look ahead to school-age and teenage years and think about the kind of messages our children receive in the big wide world. There will be opportunity to consider what kind of human beings we hope our children will be.

3: LIVE AND INTERACTIVE —RELATIONSHIP!

Please read these notes ahead of time and use them to ensure that you are well-prepared for leading the session.

Key concept:
Loving relationship

Theological basis:
We were made for God and it is foolish to neglect the spiritual aspect of our nature. We all worship something. The thing that we worship will determine the kind of person that we become. God is a loving Father to all who turn to Him for help or refuge. He is also in charge of the universe and utterly trustworthy.

Gospel opportunity:
Where do we get our values? The Christian faith provides the only absolute foundation for the kind of attributes and virtues to which we aspire for our children. It must be worth investigating whether the claims made by Jesus Christ are true. Christianity is about a relationship with Jesus Christ. Those who trust Him become members of His family. He looks forward to receiving His family in heaven.

Preparing for Session 3
• **Evaluation:** Review the previous session and think about how effective it was.

  • *Did people seem happy and comfortable?*

  • *Did people seem to understand what was taught?*

  • *Did the session run according to schedule? If not, what were the problems? Eg: Did the break take longer than expected? Did people take up time with questions? Did the presentations go on too long?*

- *Were you able to make use of any gospel opportunities?*

Resources: Make sure you have a few extra copies of the Study Guide for people who have forgotten to bring their copy to the session.

- As this is the final session, remember to have sufficient evaluation forms available for everyone to complete, and also details of any further courses or events that you would like to advertise eg: *Question and Answer panel* (see p12 of Leader's Guide); *Christianity Explored* etc. (If you are doing the 6-session version of the course, do this at the beginning of Session 6.)

Assistance: Check that you have organised people to help with welcoming and refreshments.

Film extract: Make sure that the film extract is set up for viewing, and that curtains or blinds can quickly be drawn, or are already closed at the beginning of the session.

Introduction and time to settle down	*5 minutes*
Film extract and discussion	*10 minutes*
Presentation E—*includes a group activity*	*20-30 minutes*
Group discussion 2	*10 minutes*
Refreshments and toilet break	*5 minutes*
Presentation F	*up to 40 minutes*
Group discussion 3	*10 minutes*
Wrap up	*10 minutes*
Total	**2 hours**

E: Myths and mistakes

- To build on what has been established in Sessions 1 and 2; namely, that it is right and good for parents to exercise loving authority over their children. This is done most effectively by giving equal importance and attention to the three parts of the 'magic triad'—communication, discipline and relationship.

- To focus on the aspect of relationship and examine how parents can maintain a healthy relationship with their children as they grow older.

- To dispel three common myths about how parents cultivate relationships with their children (see Presentation E: p24 of Study Guide).

- To reflect on the messages that children receive (not only from their parents but from other less helpful sources), which will inform their values.

- To introduce the idea that each child is a worshipper, and that what they worship will inform their values.

F: Virtues and values

- To challenge parents to think about what their own values are—and which ones they want to pass on to their children (see Group discussion 2: p26 of Study Guide).

- To think about how parents can provide healthy intellectual, physical, spiritual and social/emotional input into their children's lives (see Presentation F: p27 of Study Guide).

- To give ideas and resources that parents can make use of to build healthy relationships with their children.

Introduction (5 minutes maximum)

Allow a couple of minutes for people to settle down and check that everyone has a copy of the Study Guide.

- Give a brief overview of Session 3

Film extract and discussion (10 minutes)

The film extract from Dead Poets Society shows the effect on an adolescent boy of the lack of any meaningful relationship between him and his parents. This is followed by a discussion in which parents are challenged about how well they really know their own children (p23 of Study Guide).

- Introduce an extract (details below) from the film *Dead Poets Society*, with a brief summary of who and where the two characters are.

   The extract: Set in an expensive boarding school in 1950s America, the story centres around the impact of a radical and exciting English teacher on the lives of a group of boys in their mid-teens. But the film is not just about the pupil-teacher relationship; it gives insight into the crucial relationship between parent and teenage son. One of the most poignant scenes in the film is a brief interchange between two of the pupils standing on a bridge in the school grounds. One boy admits to the other that it is his birthday and the two of them discuss the present he has received from his parents.

   'What did you get?' asks his friend.

   'They gave me this desk set.'

   There is a pause and then the friend comments with cheerful irony,

   'Yeah, well, who would want a baseball, or a car, when they could have a desk set?'

   They laugh and then the birthday boy adds, with a real note of sadness:

   'The thing is, they gave me the same one last year.'

   Both boys consider the implication of this unhappy fact and are aware of the lack of attention, the lack of interest that it denotes. And these are parents who are paying big bucks for their son's education. But the repeated present, so carelessly sent, has the message: 'We don't really care to know you' written all over it.

The scene ends with a note of rebellious fun.

'Do you know – this desk set, it's kind of aero-dynamic; it wants to fly!'

And they throw it off the bridge and laugh as it scatters on the ground and in the wind.

'Don't worry,' says the friend. *'You'll get another one next year.'*

Group discussion 1

Talk around your table about how well you know your child. See if you can answer these questions:

- What did you give him/her last birthday?
- What is his/her favourite food?
- What does he/she like best at school?
- What worries your child?
- Where would he/she want to spend an ideal day out?

Presentation E: Myths and mistakes (30 minutes max)

This presentation begins by challenging parents to make a priority of keeping a healthy relationship with their children. Three popular myths about what promotes relationships—the myths of quality time, the importance of the 'educational' and over-valuing material things—are examined and debunked.

• •

Gospel opportunity: Parents will be faced with the need to review all their values and the reasons why those values must be right. This may be the first time that some people have ever been asked to think about and express their values, or what they consider to be good values. It's a great opportunity to get people to think about why they have the values they do. Are they just following the fashions of the age or the traditions of their upbringing? Could they defend the rightness of these values if they were challenged by others—including their children? The Christian faith provides the only absolute foundation for the kind of virtues and values which we want our children to have.

Forgiveness is a good example to use at this point, because it is mostly seen as a good thing and yet it is incredibly difficult for most people to put into practice. Christians don't believe in forgiveness because it is better for us or for our society, or because that is how we were brought up, or even because we like the idea of forgiveness. We believe in forgiveness because God is a forgiving God. Our Creator has decreed that forgiveness is right and good. But more that that—He has made it possible, at great cost to Himself, for each of us to be forgiven of far more things done against Him than we have ever suffered from others. This illustrates how, in the Bible, right and wrong doesn't depend on who has power or what is in fashion or how I feel—it depends on God, our Creator, who is eternal, unchanging and always faithful. There is no surer foundation for values than that!

Encourage parents to see that having a child—with all that is involved in experiencing the miracle of new birth, and recognising the daunting task that lies ahead—presents the perfect opportunity to explore what they believe and why.

••

Outline of Presentation E
Introductory comments

- Remind your group of the subjects dealt with in Session 2—communication and discipline.

- Remind them of the saying: *Rules without relationship lead to rebellion.*

- Introduce the main topic of Session 3, which is relationship, the third point of the magic triad.

- Point out that the most excellent discipline strategy will fail if the parent's relationship with the child is poor.

- Describe what is involved in growing a relationship.

- **Illustration:** *It is not like plumbing in a washing machine, which can work for years without you giving it any attention. It is more like a pot plant on the kitchen windowsill: if you ignore it, it will die.*

- Explain that problems in the teenage years nearly always come down to a failure in relationship.

- **Illustration:** *A parent may recall how sweet James was when he was a little boy, and how well they got on—going to the park, making Airfix models, reading Asterix together... But now...!! What went wrong was that the parent did not work at keeping the relationship alive as the child developed different interests that were more difficult for their parents to share. Now that James is fourteen, because the relationship has become so poor, communication has been reduced to grunts, and discipline is impossible to maintain.*

- Tell your group that the first thing needed in this session is to get rid of three common myths about relationships between parents and children—myths that lead many well-intentioned, loving parents to make fundamental mistakes (refer to p24 of the Study Guide).

1. THE MYTH OF QUALITY TIME

Examples:

'We're going to Bognor to spend some quality time with the children'

'I've taken the afternoon off to spend quality time with the children.'

- *Your example / illustration:*

- Pose the question: *How much time do you spend with your children?*

- Point out that parents can only offer their children time, rather than quality time, because the quality of the time spent together is only recognised with hindsight. What the children will remember years later as a highlight is not something that parents can accurately plan for.

- Explain that there is nothing wrong with planning holidays and taking time off, but highlight what very often what lies behind statements like those above—the wishful thinking that you can maintain a healthy relationship with your child by having a week in Bognor, or by ring-fencing an hour a week in your diary.

- Stress that a growing child is not a car to be serviced or a lawn to be mown.

- Draw attention to a second problem with the idea of 'quality time'—the fact that because it is intense, it can become artificial and even unhealthy.

- **Illustration:** *Separated or divorced parents who have access to their children once a week are well aware of this problem. Taking a child to the zoo or to McDonald's is not real life; it does not replace the 'everyday-ness' of meeting them from school, having breakfast together, bedtime stories, finding the lost and vital bit of Lego etc, which are the stuff of a real relationship.*

- Encourage parents to spend time side by side with their children, doing ordinary things. Give some suggestions:

  - Shared household chores are superb at developing a sense of belonging;

  - Parallel activities in the same room are equally good. You don't always have to be talking or letting the child set the agenda, although there is, of course, also a place for that in a healthy relationship.

  - *Your suggestion / illustration:*

- Point out that just by functioning around each other, parents will be giving their children a message of easy-going friendship, availability and accessibility.

- Emphasise that in a family where parents and children spend a large amount of normal time together, moments that are later remembered as quality time will occur. This will probably not be at our convenience, but the day a teenage son or daughter initiates a heart-to-heart talk about things that really matter is precious. Stress that such times cannot be planned in a diary.

2. THE MYTH OF 'EDUCATIONAL'

- Pose the question: *How do you talk to your child?*

- Point out to your group that some parents only ever talk to their children in a restricted way that fails to treat the child as a whole person.

Examples:

   'Would you like more orange juice?' (Cafeteria mode)

'Ah – lovely fresh air! Did you know that air contains 78% nitrogen?' (Tutorial mode)

• *Your example / illustration:*

• Explain that a trip to a good museum or other educational centre can certainly be enjoyable and have great value for parents and children, but not every day of the holidays.

• You could mention the concept of 'paranoid parenting', (a phrase first coined for the title of a book by Frank Furedi, professor of sociology at Kent University, written in 2004). One of the symptoms of the rise of paranoid parenting, he says, is the feeling that parents have to be continually organising activities for their children, or interacting with them, or both. One effect is that parents come to dread school holidays, and a significant proportion feel that the summer holidays are too long.

• Encourage parents to spend time just chilling out with their children or having fun together. Give some suggestions:

  • With young children, weekend mornings in the parental bed are a good example of this sort of thing. Eg: the aim of the game 'King of the Bed' is to be the last person on the bed, having forced the other members off (along with most of the bedding)! Families will have their own variations on this theme; the main ingredients are noise and horseplay, and just getting physical.

  • Non-organised and spontaneous activities are great. Encourage parents to let their children potter about in the house, garden, street or park, where the parent's role is supportive in a minimal supervisory sense.

  • Use imagination to make ordinary events fun. Indoor picnics on wet August afternoons, an impromptu game of cricket down the hall, a rummage among the rubbishy 5p toys at the jumble sale in the scout hut; these can generate hours of fun and strengthen the bond between parents and children.

  • *Your example / illustration:*

3. THE MYTH OF THINGS

• Pose the question: *Is life all about what you possess?*

• Point out that young children certainly do not think so. Eg: watch the pleasure a child can find in a cardboard box, some clothes pegs or a few saucepans.

• Underline that all loving parents like to give to their children, and may find buying for the children even more fun than buying for themselves. But emphasise that we need to be careful about overloading our children with things.

• Explain that although we may see giving as an expression of our immense love for our children, we must realise that the message of love is not proportional to the price of the gift.

• Warn your group about how frequent extravagance in this area can merely train them to be grasping little materialists.

• **Illustration:** *If you have none of your own, use the following:*
  The author was shocked to see her toddler son, on arriving at Grandma's, ignoring her welcome and reaching for her handbag instead. He knew there would be something for him in it, and she had unwittingly taught him, through her eagerness to give, to value the gifts more than the giver.

• *Your illustration:*

• Stress that materialistic behaviour in our children is the result of parents buying them too much. Point out that this teaches them to expect much from material things, which not only sets them up for disappointment, but actually diminishes the thrill of receiving gifts.

• **Illustration:** *Some people known to the author took great pleasure in buying their children expensive gifts at Christmas, Easter, birthdays and for any excuse in between. One Christmas Day, their ten-year-old son ripped the wrapping paper off the costly state-of-the-art electronic game they had purchased, pulled a disappointed face and then looked up at his parents with annoyance and said: 'Is this it?' They knew then what they had done.*

- Give your group a good principle to bear in mind when shopping for presents for their children—the principle of **one less**. This means that whatever they have planned to buy, they should take it down one notch. Instead of the super-duper set, get the super one. Their child will not know, and it will help them keep the spending within bounds.

- Reassure parents that when their children are grown up and recall their childhoods, it can be guaranteed that the golden moments they remember will have little to do with things that were bought for them, but everything to do with the things they did together as a family. Emphasise that **things rarely enhance a relationship**; it is shared experiences that count.

- To underline this point and conclude the first part of this session, you may like to refer to a John Denver song called *Matthew*, an endearing portrait of a happy man:

   Joy was just a thing that he was raised on;
   Love was just a way to live and die;
   Gold was just a windy Kansas wheat field;
   Blue was just a Kansas summer sky.

Group discussion 2 (10 minutes maximum)

Refer to page 26 of the study guide and pose the question: *What kind of person do we want our children to be?*

- Remind your group of one of the Bible's definitions of a child that we looked at in Session 1—an arrow into the future—and stress the responsibility that this fact places on a parent, to set the direction for the future moral and social development of their child.

- Point out how important it is for us as parents to examine and sort out what our values are. You can mention that the Bible is a fantastic source of many values that are prized in our society. Why not take the opportunity to recommend that parents spend time getting to know the Bible better?

Break (5 minutes maximum)

Presentation F: Values and virtues (40 minutes max)

Refer to page 26 of the Study Guide.

Outline of Presentation F

Introductory comments:

* List the kinds of virtues that most parents will probably have put on their list of things that they would like to produce in their child: kind, hardworking, purposeful, cheerful, loving, independent, modest, confident, courageous, truthful, reliable, etc.

* Ask whether anyone put being rich or 'drop-dead gorgeous' on their list. Stress that most of us know that these things are of little ultimate importance.

* But pose the fundamental question that parents need to consider: *How is your child going to develop the sort of characteristics that we all recognise as important, rather than those that we all know are ultimately of little value?*

* Explain that, to start with, parents must recognise two things about their children— and about all children—that will affect how they develop their own characteristics and values:

1. Your child is a receiver

2. Your child is a worshipper

1. YOUR CHILD IS A RECEIVER

* Describe what is meant here by the word 'receiver'—used in the sense of a radio receiver. Point out that from the day of birth, a child's wonderful and complex brain is picking up messages, from inside the home and from outside the home. They include the things that a parent tells them by words and by actions, but as a child grows, he or she is receiving all sorts of other messages as well.

* **Illustration:** *If you have none of your own, use the following:*
  1. Here is an example, reported in the Daily Telegraph in March 2005.
  'Now girls as young as five years old think they have to be slim to be popular. This is the claim of research published in the British Journal of Developmental Psychology.' The study, conducted among 5 to 8-year-olds in South Australia, showed that girls as young as 5 are unhappy with their bodies and want to be thinner. Most girls thought that being slim would make them more popular. Where did they get that idea?'

2. *Panorama in November 2004 investigated children and designer clothes. The programme reported and showed boys and girls of junior school age, in some cases encouraged by their parents, who were not particularly affluent, shopping for designer labels. Viewers saw groups of little children who could not yet read, recognising with ease certain commercial labels, like Nike for example. There were little girls who said they would not be friends with anyone who wore clothes bought at Tesco or Asda.*

- Emphasise that a child is a receiver of all kinds of messages, and not all of them are good.
- Go through the following list of messages that are commonly communicated in our society. Note the variety of sources for all these messages and the fact that many of them contradict each other.
  - **You are special**—parents communicate this by words, smiles and hugs, but on the other hand...
  - **you are just a random collection of neurons and chemicals**—that is the message of evolutionary science, which denies that any particular individual has any absolute significance.
  - **You are responsible**—parents and teachers will frequently aim to instil a sense of responsibility and accountability, but on the other hand...
  - **you can't help it**—a whole therapy culture surrounds people with the message that they are victims of someone or something else, whether because of their genes, other people or circumstances. All their troubles are someone else's fault and they have a right to expect help, support or even compensation.
  - **Be kind**—many parents will seek to instil at the very least a 'do-as-you-would-be-done-by' attitude to others, but on the other hand....
  - **do what feels right**—there is a very strong message in our culture that a person should be 'free' to choose what feels right for him, regardless of the impact of that choice on others.
  - **You are loved for yourself**—instinctively, we recognise that people have value regardless of how they perform, but on the other hand....
  - **Perform well**—the message of the continual emphasis on tests and assessments is that a person's worth is directly proportional to their performance.

- **Everything must be fun**—the emphasis on entertainment in our culture can mean that a child expects to find everything enjoyable; if it is not fun or if it is perceived as boring, it must definitely be rejected. On the other hand....

- **life is full of all sorts of pain, troubles and difficulties**—should these always be avoided? Or is there some truth in the idea commonly taught in previous generations that there is no gain without pain?

- Warn parents that they shouldn't immediately blame harmful messages on television or peer groups. Point out that we adults are quite capable of holding contradictory views; maybe we ourselves are not quite sure what we believe about what a human being is, and how we should live. So it is quite possible that these conflicting messages are also communicated from inside the home.

2. YOUR CHILD IS A WORSHIPPER

- Point out that people love to worship, and that this characteristic is something unique to humans, which is not seen in the animal kingdom.

- Describe what is meant by worship, by using illustrations.

Illustration: *If you have none of your own, use the following:*

1. Some of you may have been present or witnessed the scenes at the Queen's Golden Jubilee celebrations in the summer of 2002—thousands of people in front of Buckingham Palace and thronging The Mall, united in something they could not define. It was worship!

2. Think of football terraces on a Saturday afternoon—what are those people doing, shouting and chanting and cheering? They are worshipping.

3. Alternatively, consider young people at a rave. They are also worshipping. The band, 'Faithless', had a track which acknowledged precisely that fact; it was called 'This is my church'.

- *Your illustration:*

- Emphasise that our children will always worship something or things. Or put it another way—something will drive them, perhaps fuelled by the messages mentioned earlier.

- List some of the things that children commonly 'worship'.

  - money

  - friends

  - admiration / approval

  - success

  - feeling good

  - new experiences

- Pose the question: *What will drive your child?* Challenge parents to be serious about thinking through the answer to this question. Stress that what their children worship now will affect the people that they become, in the same way that we are all shaped by the things we worship.

THINKING ABOUT VALUES

- Give the group some examples of the kinds of questions that they should be asking:

  - *Will I have them shaped by advertisements?*

  - *Will I have them crave supermodel looks?*

  - *How will these influences fit in with my list of desirable values?*

- Warn parents that they will need to be serious about working out what their values are, if they are serious about raising their children well.

- You could quote here from a judge, in his foreword to a book called *Crime and the Civil Society*, in which he says:

  'The important thing is to deflect and deter young people from starting a life of crime, to catch those who do commit a crime and to deal with them appropriately. The task can be summed up by three Ps: parenting, policing and punishment. Many would add a fourth: piety. Selfishness is the forerunner of every criminal act.'

- Point out that parents today need to teach their children to be unselfish, but we are living in a society which has abandoned its Christian heritage, and therefore its high regard for unselfishness. The problem for parents is that their children may well say to them: 'Why shouldn't I be selfish? Why can't I look out for the best deal for myself?'

- Explain that our generation still understands and appreciates Christian virtues because we are still freeloading from a Christian heritage, even although many people are secular humanists, who have no allegiance to the Christian faith.

- Outline the problem that faces conscientious parents today—often we know the kind of human being we want to raise, and the sorts of values that we want to instil in your children. And yet, in a society that has largely abandoned the Christian faith, we have no reason to recommend those values, except for the fact that we like them—an opinion that our children may well decide to disagree with.

- Challenge parents with the need to review all their values and the reasons why those values must be right. Encourage them to see that having a child—with all that is involved in experiencing the miracle of new birth, and recognising the daunting task that lies ahead—presents the perfect opportunity to explore what they believe and why.

- Mention that this course is based on Bible teaching, and recommend that people investigate what the Bible says to us about our place in the universe and how we can find peace with God, or if there really is anything in this Jesus that Christians are always talking about. (This may be the opportunity to advertise details of any evangelistic course run by your church.)

- **Summarise** what has been covered so far: parents who want to instil values need to understand that their child is...

    1. A RECEIVER—what will he or she make of those messages pounding upon him or her?

    2. A WORSHIPPER—what will he or she worship?

BALANCE THE INPUT

Refer to p27 of the Study Guide

- Reassure parents that despite the failings of modern society, as parents they can still have considerable input into the way that their children come to think of themselves, the world, right and wrong, etc.

- But point out that if parents want to raise a well-rounded child, they will need to balance their input among four important areas of growth.

- Mention that although the Bible tells us very little about the childhood and growing years of Jesus of Nazareth, there is one intriguing sentence that illustrates the four areas of growth that parents need to keep in mind:

  'Jesus Christ grew in wisdom and stature, and in favour with God and men.'

  - **Wisdom**—intellectual development

  - **Stature**—physical development

  - **Favour with God**—spiritual development

  - **Favour with men**—social development

- Explain that, at any given time, it is a good idea as parents to review what is needed, where the gaps are and whether there is a correct balance between all four areas.

  - **Intellectual development:** this includes the encouragement of such things as curiosity, speech, language, literacy, numeracy, general knowledge in many areas, discernment, asking the right questions, how to learn and go on learning.

  - **Physical development:** this includes co-ordination, agility, dexterity, dressing, toilet training , blowing nose, cleanliness, games, healthy eating, control of sexual drives, exercise.

  - **Spiritual development:** this includes awe and wonder, and consideration of the big questions such as…Who made me? Who am I? How shall I respond to challenging experiences? What about death? What things are important? How shall I live?

    Point out that parents might think they are neutral on such matters and do not wish to influence their child in any way. But they need to understand that neutrality on these matters is a myth. Their refusal to discuss such questions is in itself a statement no less forceful than that of a parent who teaches her child to repeat the Apostles' Creed by rote.

  - **Social development:** this includes skills such as relating, sharing, participating, serving. It embraces the teaching of manners, thoughtfulness, losing and winning at games, how to be a friend, and how to deal with peer-group pressure.

- Draw attention to the fact that both parents and children have natural tendencies which make some types of behaviour easier or more difficult than others. Encourage people to accept this, but not to pander to it. For example, the shy introvert has to learn courteous behaviour, and the mathematical genius has to learn to tie his shoelaces.

- Reassure parents that all this input is going on while they are developing and maintaining a healthy relationship with their child.

- Point out that while balancing parental input like this probably sounds an impossible task, there are plenty of resources available, most of them useful for both input and relationship at any age or stage.

- Introduce your group to the following list of resources that can help them build relationships with their children.

THE RESOURCES:

1. Games—mention indoor and outdoor, improvised or packaged.

2. Joint activities and projects—eg: shared chores. Point out that helping with chores should be expected by any parent of a child. Stress that although allowing a child to help with a task will significantly lengthen the time that it takes, the rewards are not only good training in life-skills, cooperation and service, but a strengthened bond between parent and child.

3. Shared stories—Reading to the children should be a daily shared pleasure, way beyond the time when they are capable of reading for themselves. Point out that this is a great way to strengthen relationships, as parent and child enter a world together and empathise with the characters in the book. It is a valuable opportunity for input as you share emotions and face trials along with the hero. What will he do? What should he do? The same thing can happen when you watch film or TV together. Favourite stories then become part of the family mythology: songs, jokes, characters, even dialogue will often be recalled between you.

4. The wider family—if you are lucky enough to have one. Not only does this offer a range of role models and a pool of skills and talents; involvement with the wider family, with all its inbuilt stories and history creates a sense of belonging, an opportunity for learning and caring across the generations, and plenty to celebrate.

5. School—At some point parents will choose a school, or will choose to home-school their own children.

- Underline the fact that if the first option is chosen, parents are merely delegating some parts of their child's education to others. Although it is an important choice, encourage parents not to get too hung up about it.

- Reassure them that convenience is a very good reason for choosing a particular school over others, since it is excellent for a child to be able eventually to get himself to school independently.

- Remind people that their child will still spend at least twice as many of his/her waking hours out of school as in it. Encourage them to protect the time they have with their child and use it well.

6. Church—Encourage parents to think about looking for a church, especially if they are worried about neglecting input into their child's spiritual development. (If they have no such fear, they are probably already involved in a church at some level).

- Emphasise that it is dangerous and unhealthy to neglect the spiritual side of a child. Mention that many observers of the explosion in drug abuse by teenagers link it to the fact that most children are now raised in a spiritual vacuum.

- Highlight the fact that many churches run wholesome, safe and enjoyable regular activities for children, which include an introduction to the Christian faith through stories from the Bible. This is a setting where children have an opportunity to think through the big questions.

- Deal with parents' fears about exposing their child to propaganda, by encouraging them to think again about the human being they hope to raise. Get them to reflect on concerns like the following:

  - Are their children more likely to learn desirable qualities from a Bible story or from adverts on television? Which would they prefer to shape their children's lives?

  - Would they rather have their teenage children go clubbing or be engaged in wholesome activities with sober, decent people who will not be exploiting them for money or sex?

7. Community facilities—eg: clubs, courses and classes, libraries, parks and sports centres.

- Warn people to beware of overloading or over-organising their children however. Encourage them to remember healthy neglect. For example, a family trip to London to see some of the sights is a great idea; but so is playing cowboys and Indians in the kitchen with the table upturned and covered with a tablecloth to make a covered wagon.

8. The family meal table—one of the most valuable resources for evaluating, balancing and contributing to input.

- Explain that this encompasses all four areas for development, as a place for debate and exchange of information; a time to teach and model healthy eating and table manners; and an opportunity for social interaction of all kinds—laughter, songs, jokes, news and stories.

- Mention that sadly, many families do not recognise the value of eating together as a family.

- *Illustration: A study in March 2000, reported in 'The Archives of Family Medicine' found that of the 16,000 school-age children questioned, less than half ate with their parents on a daily basis.*

- Suggest some reasons for this disturbing trend. In many families, the children are fed separately, with a trough, as it were, placed before them. Some eat in front of the television or in their rooms. Stress that the same families are frequently surprised to find that relationships are strained and communication is minimal.

- Encourage parents to make eating together as a family a daily priority. Point out that it is even worth adjusting work routines to preserve this simple and beautiful way of maintaining relationships with their children.

9. Routines—The setting up of routines is not only excellent for discipline, it is also a wonderful way of identifying ourselves as a family. It is a way of saying: 'This is what we do or what we are'.

- Note that there are daily routines associated with bedtimes or school or hygiene; there are weekly ones, like attendance at church or some other regular shared activity; there are annual ones, which occur with the seasons. Encourage people to establish within their family traditions which are unique and personal— like the way they spend Christmas, for example.

10. **Surprises**—Remind parents to let routines occasionally give way to surprises: crazy things like getting up early to see the sunrise, going out for breakfast, appearing dressed as pirates at the tea-table, etc. Point out that these things will build a bank of memories.

CONCLUSION

1. Parenting is a burden

- Point out that parenting is not all 'picnics in the park'. As parents, the people in your group carry a responsibility much heavier than their children.

- Remind parents that life does not always turn out as they hope: dreams are shattered, hopes are unfulfilled.

- Mention that there are many variables they may hope to control as a parent, especially in the area of input that has been examined this session, but warn them that two things are beyond the control of all of us:

  1. **The future:** Emphasise that we do not know what will happen. For example, a parent may say to their child: 'I will always be here for you', but they may not be, and they cannot guarantee it. You might take this opportunity to briefly mention Jesus Christ—there is only one person who has ever said truly: 'I will be with you always' and that is Jesus Christ. Suggest that perhaps that is another reason for people to find out about him, both themselves and their child.

  2. **Our children's responses:** Point out that parents cannot control how their children will respond to their parenting. For all their good intentions and careful training, love and guidance, their child, as a responsible agent, may at some point rebel and live a life which is quite opposite to what their parents had in mind.

- Take this opportunity to mention how you personally have been helped and encouraged by knowing that God is your Father, and by the fact that He knows only too well the pain of rejection by those to whom He has given everything.

- At this point, you could remind people, or briefly tell them, the story about the prodigal son in the Bible, who freeloaded from his father and then took off to squander everything he had received.

- Point out that God knows how it feels to be rejected, and that He cares.

- Mention the great comfort that you gain from being able to entrust your children to a loving and sovereign God.

2. Parenting is exquisite

- Express the hope that this course has helped your group to see that, despite the hard work involved, raising children is a delightful privilege.

- Reassure them that each one is perfectly capable and equipped to raise delightful human beings.

- Encourage them to keep their priorities on:

  - the inner, not the outer;

  - the doing and being, not the having;

  - the long term, not the short-term.

- Encourage them to enjoy the assignment God has given them!

Group Discussion 3 (10 minutes maximum)

Refer to p28 of the Study Guide and introduce the group discussion questions.

Discuss the ways in which you find parenting an exquisite burden. Make some decisions about how you are going to enhance and improve your relationship with your child or children.

Closing comments and evaluation (10 minutes)

Refer to p25 and 29 of the Study Guide and draw attention to the questions. These are for people to think about at home (preferably both parents together).

- Encourage people to fill in and return the evaluation form, and to sign up for any course or events that you may have advertised.

PUTTING PARENTING TO BED
Evaluation Form

Please complete and then detach this page from the book and give it to the leader of the course.

Please tick the appropriate boxes.

Which sessions have you attended?

☐ The trouble with parenting   ☐ The big D-word   ☐ Live and interactive

- *What was your rating of the course ?*

	Poor	Satisfactory	Good
Content			
Style			
Timing			

- *What did you find most helpful?*

- *What did you / will you try to put into practice?*

- *Any further comments?*

- *Were you surprised to hear that the Bible contains guidance relevant for parenting today?*
  ☐ **Yes** ☐ **No**

- *Would you be interested in hearing more about the Christian faith?* ☐ **Yes** ☐ **No**

If you would be interested in attending a short course exploring the Christian faith, please write your contact details below.

Name: _____

Contact number: _____

Please use the back for any other comments you would like to add.
All information is treated with the strictest confidence.

your notes

your notes

your notes

your notes

your notes

your notes